REFORMED PIETY

COVENANTAL AND EXPERIENTIAL

JOEL R BEEKE
STEPHEN G MYERS

Published by **EP Books** (Evangelical Press), Registered Office: 140 Coniscliffe Road, Darlington, Co Durham DL3 7RT

admin@epbooks.org

www.epbooks.org

EP Books are distributed in the USA by: JPL Books, 3883 Linden Ave. S.E., Wyoming, MI 49548

order@jplbooks.com

www.jplbooks.com

ISBN 978-1-78397-248-7

ePub ISBN 978-1-78397-249-4

Scripture quotations are from the King James version of the Holy Bible.

CONTENTS

FOREWORD

My great lamentation, utterly sincere and grievous, is the weakness of my Christian piety or personal godliness during that long ministry of mine, for over half a century. How my preaching would have been more awakening and my presence far more fruitful if there had only been deeper and more transparent Christlikeness in my life! I am understanding at the end of my days what Robert Murray M'Cheyne understood in his twenties, that the greatest need of his congregation was his own piety. That is where this little book is taking us, to the closing words of the chapter on *Experiential Piety* that are very convicting words, but essential words if you will hear them:

> John Boys (1571–1625) captured this truth when he quipped, "He doth preach most, that doth live best." Do we think that we will ignite others with the love of God if we are not burning and shining lights ourselves? John Owen (1616–1683) said that a minister needs an "experience of the power of the things we preach to others." Owen wrote, "No man preaches that sermon so well to others who does not preach it first to his own heart... Unless he finds the power of it in his own

heart, he cannot have any ground of confidence that it will have power in the hearts of others."

— QUOTED FROM PAGE 30 BELOW

This is not merely a historical lecture on Reformed piety, important as that would be, though there are such elements necessarily in these pages. Its focus is not cerebral, on our understanding. The original was given to move the audience and those who would later read it towards Reformed experiential living reflecting something of the Christian's affection for God, loving Him with all his being, a servant truly on flame for his Lord, who cries, "For me to live is Christ"—who is presenting his body as a living sacrifice to God, who like John the Baptist has an awakening ministry, as a burning and a shining light. Correct theological understanding is essential, insights from the history of redemption are immensely helpful to understanding the Scripture, a blameless moral character is required in any who would stand in the place of God and declare His word, but most needful of all is a close walk with God, a consecration of all we are to all that Jesus Christ is. That must be the one thing we do as Christians, not talking about it, or longing for it, but making progress in appropriating it each day of our lives, in the pulpit, in the home, visiting the congregation, and before our neighbors. In this way, the words of this little book will help you to be a better disciple in our short and uncertain earthly pilgrimage.

Geoff Thomas

INTRODUCTION

During the five-hundredth anniversary of the Reformation in 2017, with all the articles, books, conferences, and tours it generated, the question was often asked: What was the Reformation all about? [1] A good case was made by some for asserting that it was primarily about the cardinal doctrine of justification by faith alone. Others argued that its primary emphasis was on the doctrine of salvation in general. Still others planted their flag on the critical issue of biblical worship, or on biblical authority versus the claims of the papacy. A key concern of the Reformation that was often passed over is that of the great revival of *biblical piety*, particularly as it manifested itself in the theology and lives of the Reformers and later, the Puritans. No one set forth the nature of biblical piety so succinctly and frequently as the great Reformer, John Calvin (1509–1564).

In this little book, I aim to accomplish four things: First, to give you a bird's eye view of what Reformed *piety* is by looking at Calvin as one of its premier magisterial representatives. Second, to examine how we understand what Reformed piety should be in relation to the covenant of grace. I wish to thank my colleague Dr. Stephen Myers (PhD), Associate Professor of Historical Studies at Puritan Reformed Theological Seminary, who did the heavy lifting on this chapter for me—hence the co-authorship of this book. Having done his doctoral dissertation on Ebenezer Erskine's covenant theology, he is eminently qualified to write this chapter. Third, to consider what Reformed piety should be in the context of Christian experience. Finally, to present some conclusions that explore the interface between these three concepts in Reformed thought: piety, covenant, and experience.

Joel R. Beeke

CALVIN'S PIETY

John Calvin's *Institutes* earned him the reputation of being the preeminent systematician of the Protestant Reformation. His achievement as an intellectual, however, is often considered in isolation from the vital spiritual and pastoral context in which he wrote his theology. For Calvin, theological understanding and practical piety, truth and usefulness, were inseparable. Theology first of all deals with knowledge—knowledge of God and of ourselves—but there is no true knowledge where there is no true piety.[1]

Pietas (piety) is one of the major themes of Calvin's theology. His theology is, as John T. McNeill said, "his piety described at length."[2] He was determined to confine theology within the limits of piety.[3] In his preface addressed to King Francis I, Calvin said that the purpose of writing the *Institutes* was "solely to transmit certain rudiments by which those who are touched with any zeal for religion might be shaped to true godliness [*pietas*]."[4]

The Latin word *pietas* was important in ancient Roman religion and culture. With respect to the gods, it denoted piety or devotion, and especially conscientiousness or scrupulousness in giving the gods their due; with respect to parents, benefactors, and one's nation or country, it denoted duty and dutifulness, affection and love, loyalty and patriotism, and many other virtues.[5] So you can see how easy it was for Latin-speaking Christians to adopt this word to denote Christian faith and faithfulness, devotion to duty, and true godliness.

For Calvin, *pietas* designates the right attitude of man toward God, which includes true knowledge, heartfelt worship, saving faith, filial fear, prayerful submission, and reverential love.[6] Knowing who and what God is (theology) informs and leads to right attitudes toward Him and produces right conduct, or doing what pleases Him (piety). Calvin wrote, "I call 'piety' that reverence joined with love of God which the knowledge of his benefits induces."[7] This love and reverence for God is a necessary concomitant to any true or right knowledge of Him and extends to all of life. Calvin said, "The whole life of Christians ought to be a sort of practice of godliness."[8]

The goal of piety, as well as the entire Christian life, is the glory of God—acknowledging and magnifying that glory that shines in God's attributes, in the structure of the universe, and in the life, death, and resurrection of Jesus Christ.[9] Glorifying God supersedes personal salvation for every truly pious person.[10] The pious man, according to Calvin, confesses, "We are God's: let us therefore live for him and die for him. We are God's: let his wisdom and will therefore rule all our actions. We are God's: let all the parts of our life accordingly strive toward him as our only lawful goal."[11]

But how do we glorify God? As Calvin wrote, "God has prescribed for us a way in which he will be glorified by us, namely, piety, which consists in the obedience of his Word. He that exceeds these bounds does not go about to honor God, but rather to dishonor him."[12] Obedience to God's Word means taking refuge in Christ for forgiveness of our sins, knowing Him through His Word, serving Him with a loving heart, doing good works in gratitude for His goodness, and exercising self-denial to the point of loving our enemies.[13] This response involves total surrender to God Himself, His Word, and His will. The motto inscribed on Calvin's seal said, "My heart I offer to Thee, O Lord, promptly and sincerely."[14] That is the desire of all who are truly pious.

Thus, for Calvin, piety involves all truth and all of life. It is comprehensive, having theological, ecclesiological, and practical dimensions.

A Theological Piety

Theologically, piety can be realized only through union and communion with Christ and partaking of all His benefits, for outside of Christ even the most religious person lives for himself.[15] Only in Christ can the pious live as willing servants of their Lord, faithful soldiers of their Commander, and obedient children of their Father.

Communion with Christ is always the result of Spirit-worked faith—a work that is more astonishing and experiential than comprehensible. Faith unites the believer to Christ by means of the Word and Spirit of God, enabling the believer to receive Christ as He is clothed in the gospel and graciously offered to us by the Father. By His Word and Spirit, God also dwells in the believer. Consequently, Calvin said, "We ought not to separate Christ from ourselves or ourselves from him," but partake of Christ by faith, for this "revives us from death to make us a new creature."[16]

By faith, believers both belong to and possess Christ, and grow in Him. From Christ they receive by faith the "double grace" or "double cure" of justification and sanctification, which together provide a twofold cleansing from sin and uncleanness.[17] Justification confers imputed purity, and sanctification produces actual purity.[18]

An Ecclesiological Piety

For Calvin, piety is nurtured in the church by the preaching of the Word, administration of the holy sacraments, and the offering of praise by singing the Psalms. God uses these three manifestations to bring about spiritual birth and growth, which happen within the church. The church is mother, educator, and nourisher of every believer, for the Holy Spirit acts in her structure and through her ministry. Under the care and instruction of the church, believers progress from spiritual infancy to adolescence to adulthood in Christ. They do not graduate from the church until they die.[19] This lifelong education is offered in a context or atmosphere of genuine piety in which believers love and care for one another under the headship of Christ. "There is a bond of fellowship," says Calvin, "when no one has sufficient for himself, but is constrained to borrow from others."[20] Piety is thus fostered by the communion of saints.[21]

As noted above, piety is nurtured in the church through the preaching of the Word, which Calvin said is our spiritual food and our medicine for spiritual health. With the Spirit's blessing, ministers are spiritual physicians who apply the Word to our souls as earthly physicians apply medicine to our bodies. The preached Word is used as an instrument to heal, cleanse, and make fruitful our disease-prone souls.[22] The Spirit, as the "internal minister," promotes piety by using the Word preached by the "external minister."[23]

Piety is also nurtured in the church through sacraments, which Calvin defined as "a testimony of divine grace toward us, confirmed by an outward sign, with mutual attestation of our piety toward him."[24] The sacraments, being the visible Word, are "exercises of piety." The sacraments confirm or strengthen our faith, make us grateful to God for His abundant grace, and are a means by which we in turn offer ourselves as a living sacrifice to God.

Lastly, piety grows through offering praise, specifically using the Psalms. Calvin viewed the book of Psalms as the canonical manual of piety, hailing it as "An Anatomy of All the Parts of the Soul." Calvin immersed himself in the Psalms for twenty-five years as a commentator, preacher, biblical scholar, and worship leader in helping compile the famous Genevan Psalter.[25] In the preface to his five-volume commentary on the Psalms, Calvin wrote: "There is no other book in which we are more perfectly taught the right manner of praising God, or in which we are more powerfully stirred up to the performance of this exercise of piety."[26]

Psalm-singing is one of the principle acts of church worship, Calvin believed. It is an extension of prayer. It is also the most significant vocal contribution of people in the service. Under the Spirit's direction, Psalm-singing tunes the hearts of believers for glory.

The Practice of Personal Piety

Although Calvin viewed the church as the nursery of piety, he also emphasized the need for personal piety. For Calvin, such piety is the heart, as well as the beginning and end, of Christian living. It is involved in numerous practical dimensions of daily Christian living, with a particular emphasis on heartfelt prayer, repentance, self-denial, cross-bearing, and obedience.[27]

Conclusion

Calvin strove to live the life of *pietas* himself—theologically, ecclesiastically, practically, and personally. Having tasted the goodness and grace of God in Jesus Christ, he exercised himself in piety by seeking to know and do God's will every day. His theology and ecclesiology worked itself out in practical, heart-felt, Christ-centered piety—piety that ultimately profoundly impacted the church, the community, and the world.[28] For Calvin and the Reformed Christians who followed after him, this piety was always grounded in the covenant of grace, for, as Calvin noted, "God's people have never had any other rule of reverence and piety" than that covenant.[29]

2

COVENANTAL PIETY

In much contemporary discussion, the word "covenantal" has become rather nebulous. For older Reformed theologians, however, "covenantal" almost always has specific reference to God's covenantal dealings with man, primarily in the covenant of grace. In the eternal, intra-trinitarian divine counsel, God purposed to redeem a specific people to Himself. The outworking of that purpose in history was first announced in the ruins of Eden in Genesis 3:15, and then progressed through God's dealings with Noah, Abraham, Moses, and David, until finally, as adumbrated by the prophets, it came to fulfilment in Christ. The Reformed have called this purpose and plan of God the covenant of grace. Seeing their redemption through this specific lens, the Reformed have articulated a "covenantal" piety—a piety that finds its content and takes its shape from the particularities of God's economy of redemption. This covenantal piety of the Reformed has been intensely relational, providing both definite ethical content and a communal dynamic.

A Piety of Relationship

In the first instance, covenantal Reformed piety always has been a piety of relationship because relationship is at the heart of covenant. As Moses declared to the Israelites on the plains of Moab, God's intention in the covenant of grace is to bring men, women, and children into a relationship with Himself (Deuteronomy 29:12–13). The Scriptures assert that relationship repeatedly and clearly via the "Immanuel principle"; through the covenant of grace, God declares, "I will be their God, and they shall be my people" (2 Corinthians 6:16; cf. Genesis 17:7; Exodus 3:15; 20:2; Ezekiel 36:28; Revelation 21:3). At bottom, then, the covenant of grace is God's method of calling and transforming a heterogeneous mass of men and women, young and old, into the people of God.[1]

The intimacy and power of this covenantal relationship between God and His people are frequent themes of Scripture, which presents God's redemptive acts as expressions not simply of His character but also the outworking of His bond with His covenant people. As covenant theology has always emphasized, the Scriptures reveal God not only as the God of grace but also as the God who names Himself through His people (Exodus 3:6), whose relationship with those people is reflected visibly in His actions (Exodus 2:23–25), who has eyed those people with favor from the beginning of time (Ephesians 1:3–6; Jeremiah 1:5; Revelation 13:8), and who accomplished the great work of redemption with those specific people in view (John 17:12). Through what the Westminster divines termed His "voluntary condescension" in the covenant of grace, God has made Himself the "blessedness and reward" of a specific people, making them, by name, the people of His covenant. God expresses the intimacy of that relationship by calling His people His children (e.g., Exodus 4:22–23; Jeremiah 31:9; Isaiah 45:11; Hosea 11:1; Romans 8:15; Galatians 3:26; 1 John 3:1).[2]

The personal nature of this covenantal relationship creates what John Murray described as "mutuality"—a dynamic of reciprocity seen in passages such as Genesis 17.[3] Expressing His sovereignty, God initiates and establishes the covenant bond between Himself and His people (vv. 4–8); the relationship resulting from it is so precious that it commands and elicits human response and invests that response with meaning (vv. 9–14). The covenantal relationship, though not between equals or peers, is by the very nature of a covenant "mutual"; never is it marked by one party being unconcerned about the actions or desires of the other. This mutuality of the believer's covenantal relationship with God does not reflect contingency in that relationship, but rather the nearness and permanency of the bond. In a similar way, human marriage relationships involve much greater mutuality than even the closest friendships, yet that mutuality grows not out of conditionality to the marriage but out of the intimacy and endurance of the relationship. When God's redemptive work is understood in terms of His covenant of grace, the Christian realizes that he is not simply partaking of an eternal good that God is offering, but rather he is in relationship with his Creator.

This covenantal relationship between God and His people has infused Reformed piety with a strongly personal character.[4] God offers Himself to us, and we offer ourselves to God. Reformed Christians have found comfort under persecution in knowing that they are adopted children of God;[5] they have written of their Savior with the rapture of personal love;[6] and they even have undertaken personal covenants to specify actions and habits through which they will seek greater nearness to the God who has saved them.[7] For the Reformed, piety is not simply conformity to a norm, it is the cultivation of a relationship. A relationship that God has initiated and that He has called them to cherish, explore, nurture, and love.

A Relationship with Ethical Content

Covenant theology provides specific ethical content for this covenant relationship and the piety it fosters in us. We are not left to discover or determine for ourselves how God is to be loved and served. Almost without exception, classical covenant theology has understood the law of God to be "the living and accurate reflection of the holiness of God."[8] In the moral law, God describes what His holiness looks like when it is lived out in the midst of human society.[9] Given this connection between the law and the divine character, it is no surprise that the Reformed also have insisted on a basic continuity of that law from the Garden of Eden to Mount Sinai to the New Testament church.[10] Thus, while some consign the moral law—as summarized in the Ten Commandments (Exodus 20)—to another time or place, Reformed Christianity has always asserted the abiding character of the law, the obligation of all men to obey it, and its usefulness as a rule of life for all who are in Christ. In the context of the covenant of grace, what God said and did at Mount Sinai is inseparably linked to what He did at Calvary, and to what He is doing today among His people. In the Decalogue, then, God was not speaking outside of or apart from His redemptive covenantal purpose that had brought Abraham's seed to Sinai in the first place.[11] Rather, in the Ten Commandments, God describes the holiness that He desired to mark the lives of those whom He has redeemed according to His covenant promise.[12] In the New Testament, it is evident that this law-defined understanding of holiness has not changed. Jesus saw His earthly ministry as establishing the law in its full spirituality rather than abolishing it (Matthew 5:17). Jesus spoke of the life He desired among His people in precisely the same way as the Old Testament had spoken of law-abiding life (Matthew 5:48; compare with Leviticus 19:2; see also 1 Peter 1:13–16). Paul called for Christians' lives to be guided by the express commandments of the moral law (Ephesians 6:1–4) that he described as "holy, and just, and good" (Romans 7:12). As the covenant holds forth exceeding great and precious promises to God's people, so also it imposes on them the obligations of faith, love, and obedience. These two parts of God's covenant of grace must not be separated. The law that once condemned them as sinners has become a rule of life to all who are saved in Christ. Reformed piety, via its covenantal structure, has definite parameters, and those parameters *are* the Ten Commandments of the covenant of grace.

The vital role of covenant theology in shaping Reformed piety around this "third use of the law" is seen in the very genesis of that terminology itself. It was Philip Melanchthon who first spoke of "the third use of the law," but Lutheran piety has tended to neglect the normative role of this third use because Lutheranism was flavored by a strong dichotomy between law and grace.[13] The Reformed, on the other hand, emphasized the unity of God's covenantal dealings under both testaments and thus, beginning with Calvin himself, they saw this third use of the law as "the principal use" thereof.[14] While there have been exceptions, Reformed piety has generally remained free from unbiblical mysticism; and, simply because it has a clear and authoritative articulation of what constitutes a life of piety, it contains inherent guardrails against both the tyranny of manmade legalism and the chaos of license.[15] What keeps us from legalism is our theology of grace. When Calvinists lose it, they become legalists and Unitarians, as some heirs of the Puritans did.

A life of devotion to the God of the covenant is a life of obedience to His moral law. Traditions devoid of these covenantal sensibilities have had much greater difficulty asserting the abiding authority of the Decalogue as the moral law. That inability to move theologically from God's work on Sinai to God's work in Zion has injected an instability into their understanding of what constitutes a life of piety. Indeed, even within the broader Reformed tradition, those communions that have downplayed the continuity of God's covenant of grace have had to use agile circumlocutions to retain the Decalogue's "principles" while relegating its form to a past era of redemptive history.[16] At its best, however, Reformed theology has articulated a robust covenant theology that keeps the Ten Commandments squarely within the lives of God's covenant people as part and parcel of the covenant of grace.

Since covenant theology has placed the Ten Commandments at the center of Reformed piety, it is no wonder that some of the most profound Reformed treatments of piety take their shape explicitly from the Ten Commandments. Expositions of the Ten Commandments have figured prominently in Reformed preaching, devotional literature, and catechesis; in every instance being taken as authoritative instruction for the Christian life.[17] This impulse has continued into the twentieth and twenty-first centuries, as Reformed accounts of piety and Christian ethics continue to take their shape self-consciously from the Ten Commandments.[18] For centuries, Reformed piety, being a covenantal piety, has been aware of the unity of God's people through the ages and thus has been able to give to each successive generation of Christians the substantial, specific, ethical content of Christian piety as expressed so clearly in the Ten Commandments. When the Psalmist declared the law of God to be his "delight" (Psalm 119:174), he spoke out of the same covenant of grace by which New Testament Christians are redeemed and thus his delight in that law remains theirs.

A Communal Dynamic

Even as Reformed piety's covenantal character has connected personal piety to God's redemptive work, it likewise has invested that piety with a self-conscious attention to the human "other." The same law that requires us to love God commands us to love our neighbor as ourselves. This other-focus has led Reformed piety to attach particular importance both to the church and to the family.

In the first instance, covenantal Reformed piety has maintained Calvin's attention to a decidedly ecclesiastical piety. Through the communion of the saints, the means of grace dispensed in public worship, and church discipline, the Reformed have understood personal piety as something that is pursued in fellowship with the body of Christ and never in isolation from the church.[19] The Immanuel principle itself establishes the importance of this commitment. The Lord's promise, "I set my tabernacle [I will dwell] among you.... I will walk among you, and will be your God, and ye shall be my people" (Lev. 26:11–12), declares that God's covenantal work is not to redeem a large number of individuals, but to redeem a *people* unto Himself. Elsewhere, the Scriptures speak of God's people as a "nation" (1 Peter 2:9) or a "church" (Revelation 2:1) or a "building" (Ephesians 2:19–22)—at every point, imagery that speaks of one composite entity rather than so many isolated individuals. The Reformed have seen the implications of this corporate identity for piety very plainly, for example, in the Fourth Commandment, by which God commands not only that His people hallow the Sabbath as a day of rest, but also make it possible for their servants and even livestock to enter into that rest.[20] Within Reformed piety, the awareness of being part of a covenant people has created a dynamic whereby growth in holiness draws one out of isolation and into the life, work, and witness of the church.

Secondly, Reformed piety gives special attention to the Christian family. Perhaps nowhere is this connection more clearly stated than in Psalm 103:17–18: "The mercy of the LORD is from everlasting to everlasting upon them that fear him, and his righteousness unto children's children; to such as keep his covenant, and to those that remember his commandments to do them." Here, David exalts God's grace and faithfulness not only to the present generation of His people, but also to their children and grandchildren, and by implication, from generation to generation, "from everlasting to everlasting." Far from being a secondary issue, Calvin saw this inter-generational steadfastness as "the principal part of the covenant."[21] The most visible result of this covenant principle is the Reformed practice of infant baptism and the implications of that sacrament for the larger communal aspects of Reformed piety.[22]

At its best, the Reformed piety embodied in infant baptism is the piety of Deuteronomy 6:6–9—a piety of inter-generational discipleship, in which the older generations live their lives driven by the desire to communicate the faith by word and action to the next generation of God's people. The younger generations are not left to cast about for answers to their most yearning questions; those questions are answered by older Christians (parents, pastors, teachers, et al.) who speak of God and apply His Word to the mundane realities of everyday life. God has promised, "I will...be a God unto thee, and to thy seed after thee" (Genesis 17:7); Reformed piety is suffused with the hope and expectation that this promise will be realized in the lives of parents' children. This inter-generational dynamic has sustained the Reformed emphasis on catechesis and family worship, in which covenant children are earnestly instructed about their need to come to personal repentance and faith in Christ, according to the covenant promises signed and sealed to them in their baptism.[23] Piety is to characterize not only individuals, but also families, as a divine institution through which our covenant-keeping God most often works.

In both of these specific manifestations—in the church and in the family—this communal dynamic to Reformed piety reinforces itself. While piety is always personal, never does it push toward isolation—ascetic, monastic, or otherwise. Rather, at every point, personal Reformed piety draws the Christian toward the "other," serving, loving, and being served and loved by the men, women, and children who comprise the one people God is redeeming through His covenant of grace.

Abuses of Covenantal Piety

While the covenantal character of Reformed piety is a glorious strength, the human heart is expert at distorting and perverting this strength, so that it becomes a weakness. Regrettably, this has been true even of Reformed covenantal piety. At various points, the personal, ethical, and communal components of that piety have been distorted and used to promote doctrinal error and spiritual neglect. In general, these abuses are the result of exalting one aspect of the covenant of grace at the expense of another. The result is an unbalanced and spiritually destructive substitute or counterfeit version of covenant theology.

In the history of Reformed Christianity, different movements have elevated the personal and devotional elements of Reformed piety and minimized the ethical and communal elements. The result has been an antinomianism that focuses on a privileged standing before God while neglecting or denying the obligations of duty, both personal and communal, that belong to it.[24] Such distortions clearly injure the very nature of piety.

Similarly destructive are those movements that prioritize Reformed piety's ethical content to the detriment of its personal component. Piety is reduced to doing one's duty in church, at home, and at large. Membership in the covenant community is taken as a guarantee of eternal life. With little or no concern for a genuine personal experience of God's grace in Christ, piety is reduced to purely external conformity to the laws of God and man, reducing true godliness to mere morality.

Such legalism, whether crass or subtle, views the law as consti-
tutive of one's relationship with God rather than as a guide or
teacher of duty to those who by faith enjoy such a relationship.
This confusion stems from a prior failure to recognize the
personal component of Reformed piety, the believer's union
with Christ through faith, and the communication of life from
Him by the indwelling Spirit, through which ethical conduct is
alone possible.[25]

While both of these distortions have appeared among the
Reformed, the most prominent and distinctive error within this
tradition has been the tendency to exalt the communal aspect
of Reformed piety above all other components. This particular
error has taken two different forms. In the first instance, some
have concluded that God's ordinary inter-generational work is
a guaranteed and effectual work. Thus, the children of
believers have been seen as necessarily regenerate. In some
versions of this error, its exponents have advocated baptismal
regeneration while others have urged that children of believers
be at least presumed to be regenerate, unless or until there is
evidence to the contrary.[26] Whatever forms the particular error
has taken, however, they share the same root. In each instance,
the communal dynamic of Reformed covenantal piety is seen
to work independently of either personal, divinely initiated
relationship or personal manifestation of ethical conformity.
The covenantal community emphasis then swallows up the
need for personal regeneration, conversion, and holiness. One
might say that these errors appeal to Psalm 103:17 ("But the
mercy of the LORD is from everlasting to everlasting upon
them that fear him, and his righteousness unto children's children") but ignore verse 18 ("to such as keep his covenant, and to
those that remember his commandments to do them"). The
communal vitality of biblical piety (v. 17) always manifests itself
in successive generations of ethically expressed personal relationships (v. 18).

The second error that has stemmed from the communal element of Reformed piety's covenantal character has been an impulse toward so-called "hyper-Calvinism," if not in doctrine then at least in practice. God's ordinary working through familial and ecclesiastical relationships has caused some Reformed Christians to focus so much on those avenues that they neglect or deny the imperative of evangelism to bring sinful men and women out of the world into a vital, experiential relationship with Himself, just as He has done through the means of family relationship and church fellowship. The church and the families belonging to it become a closed society, existing by and for themselves. Such churches are not as cities set upon a hill so they cannot be hid; their members are candles put under a bushel, and not on a candlestick, "to give light unto all" (Matthew 5:14–15), thus defeating the very purpose for which Christ builds His church in the world.

Summary of Covenantal Piety

In both its most luminous strengths and its most persistent errors, Reformed piety has been a covenantal piety. In its true form, Reformed piety organically emerges from that covenant of grace by which God first redeems His people, gathers them out of the world, enfolds them in His church, and then calls them to—and gives them the spiritual capacities for—a life of devotion to Him. Such a life became known over time as a life of experiential piety—hence the intimate connection between piety, covenant, and genuine Christian experience.

EXPERIENTIAL PIETY

Until the mid-nineteenth century, Calvin and the Reformed were often labeled "experimental" or "experiential."[1] The term *experimental* comes from the Latin *experimentum*, meaning "trial." It is derived from the verb *experior*, meaning "to try, prove, or put to the test." That verb also can mean "to find or know by experience," thus leading to the word *experientia*, meaning "knowledge gained by experiment." Calvin used *experiential* and *experimental* interchangeably, since both words indicate the need for measuring our "knowledge gained by experience" by the rule or standard of Scripture.

Reformed churches have historically regarded the ministry of the Word and the work of the Holy Spirit as inseparable from one another. This coupling of Word and Spirit has its practical result in the primacy of preaching to plant and cultivate experiential piety. Without the appointed means, we cannot expect to attain the desired end, so both must be discussed together.

Experiential piety arises when, by God's grace, the truth of God's Word is applied to the whole range of the believer's personal experience, including his relationship with God, and with his family, the church, and the world around him.[2] Experiential preaching seeks to explain biblically what the Reformers called vital religion: how a sinner must be stripped of his self-righteousness, driven to Christ alone for salvation, and led to the joy of simple reliance on Christ. It aims further, to show how a redeemed sinner encounters the plague of indwelling sin, battles against temptation, endures trials, suffers affliction, and gains victory by faith in Christ.

God's Word must be preached not only biblically, doctrinally, and practically, but also experientially, for it is "the power of God unto salvation" (Romans 1:16) that transforms men and nations. Such preaching is transforming because it faithfully proclaims the gospel, accurately describes the vital experience of the children of God (Romans 5:1–11), clearly explains the marks and fruits of the saving grace necessary for a believer (Matthew 5:3–12; Galatians 5:22–g23), and sets before believer and unbeliever alike their eternal futures (Revelation 21:1–9), calling all to faith in Christ as the only Savior.

When God's Spirit is pleased to use such preaching, Reformed divines have noted that the resulting piety has the following characteristics.

1. Piety Based on the Written Word

Reformed piety is biblical piety. Calvin said, "In order that true religion may shine upon us, we ought to hold that it must take its beginning from heavenly doctrine and that no one can get even the slightest taste of right and sound doctrine unless he be a pupil of Scripture. Hence, there also emerges the beginning of true understanding when we reverently embrace what it pleases God there to witness of himself."[3] Reverence for God entails reverence for His Word. Calvin warned, "The Holy Spirit so inheres in his truth, which he expresses in Scripture, that only when its proper reverence and dignity are given to the Word does the Holy Spirit show forth his power."[4]

Therefore, Reformed experiential piety springs up where the seed of the Word is sown. According to Isaiah 8:20, all of our beliefs, including our experiences, must be tested by holy Scripture. That is really what the word *experimental* intends to convey. Just as a scientific experiment tests a given hypothesis against a body of evidence, so experimental preaching examines experience in the light of the teaching of the Word of God.

Building on the written Word preserves experiential Christianity from unbiblical mysticism. Mysticism separates experience from the Word, whereas historic Reformed conviction demands biblical and experiential faith. One scholar writes of "the interdependence of piety and theology" in the Reformed tradition: "The specific response of man to God is determined by theology.... Theology gives piety its objective content."[5] That kind of scripturally informed godliness is essential to the health and prosperity of the church.

2. Piety Centered on Christ

The great theme and controlling contour of experiential preaching and piety is Jesus Christ, for He is the supreme focus, prism, and goal of God's revelation. Therefore, a true Calvinistic preacher must be "determined not to know any thing...save Jesus Christ, and him crucified" (1 Corinthians 2:2). The Puritans considered Christ to be the jewel of every sermon. William Perkins (1558–1602) said that the heart of all preaching is "to preach one Christ, by Christ, to the praise of Christ."[6] Cotton Mather (1663–1728) put it this way: "Exhibit as much as you can of a glorious Christ. Yea, let the motto upon your whole ministry be: *Christ is all.*"[7]

Since the Spirit always testifies of Jesus Christ, sound exegesis finds Christ not only in the New Testament, but also in

the Old. It was said in the ancient world that all roads led to
Rome; so the preaching of all texts today must lead ultimately
to Christ. Jesus Himself says, "Search the scriptures; for in
them ye think ye have eternal life: and they are they which
testify of me" (John 5:39). Likewise, when He meets with His
disciples following His resurrection, Jesus says, "These are the
words which I spake unto you, while I was yet with you, that all
things must be fulfilled, which were written in the law of
Moses, and in the prophets, and in the psalms, concerning me"
(Luke 24:44).

Such preaching teaches that Christ, the living Word (John
1:1) and the very embodiment of truth, must be experientially
known and embraced. It proclaims the need for sinners to
experience who God is in His Son. As John 17:3 says, "This is
life eternal, that they might know thee the only true God, and
Jesus Christ, whom thou hast sent." The word *know* in this text,
as often in other parts of the Bible, does not indicate casual
acquaintance, but knowledge in the context of a deep, abiding
relationship, "that knowledge which forms us anew into the
image of God from faith to faith," as Calvin said.[8] Experiential
piety seeks the intimate, personal, transforming knowledge of
God in Christ.

3. Piety Applied to Practical Life

While Calvinistic preaching is rooted in grammatical historical
exegesis, it also involves spiritual, practical, and experiential
application. In 1 Corinthians 2:10–16, Paul says that good
exegesis is a spiritual endeavor. Exegesis offers sound analysis
of the words, grammar, syntax, and historical setting of Scripture. Experiential preaching does not minimize these aspects
of interpretation, but neither is it content with them. A
minister who presents only the grammatical and historical
meaning of God's Word may be lecturing or discoursing, but he

is not preaching. The Word must be applied spiritually. Spiritual exegesis is thus Christological, and, through Christ, it will be theological, bringing all glory to the triune God.

Reformed piety is essentially nothing but biblical truth applied to all of life. Robert Burns (1789–1869) defined such religion as "Christianity brought home to men's business and bosoms." He went on to say that the principle on which it rests is that "Christianity should not only be known, and understood, and believed, but also felt, and enjoyed, and practically applied."[9] Charles Bridges (1794–1869) called for sermons that follow "the method of perpetual application."[10] In this regard, Bridges stood squarely in the Reformed and Puritan tradition summarized by the Westminster Directory for the Public Worship of God, which says:

> He [the preacher] is not to rest in general doctrine, although never so much cleared and confirmed, but to bring it home to special use, by application to his hearers: which albeit it prove a work of great difficulty to himself, requiring much prudence, zeal, and meditation, and to the natural and corrupt man will be very unpleasant; yet he is to endeavour to perform it in such a manner, that his auditors may feel the word of God to be quick and powerful, and a discerner of the thoughts and intents of the heart; and that, if any unbeliever or ignorant person be present, he may have the secrets of his heart made manifest, and give glory to God.[11]

The Westminster divines identified six kinds of application: *instruction* in doctrine, *confutation* of error, *exhortation* to obedience, *dehortation* against sin, *comfort* for the afflicted, and giving *"notes of trial"* for self-examination.[12] We might add a seventh: *doxology* or showing forth the praises of God.

4. Piety Probed by Spiritual Discernment

Preaching that cultivates piety, Reformed divines believed, must discriminate, not between the two genders or the various ethnic groups, but between the distinct spiritual states and conditions of human beings. It clearly defines the difference between a believer and an unbeliever, opening the kingdom of heaven to one and shutting it against the other.

The Heidelberg Catechism identifies "preaching" and "Christian discipline" as the keys of the kingdom of heaven. Referencing Matthew 16:19, it says that "by these two, the kingdom of heaven is opened to believers and shut against unbelievers."[13] Jesus Christ modeled this kind of preaching in the Sermon on the Mount, for example, in the manner that His introduction, the Beatitudes, summarized the spiritual marks of the true member of Christ's kingdom (Matthew 5:3–12), while in His conclusion He posts a solemn warning for those who do not hear and obey the Word. If our religion is not experiential, we will perish—not because experience itself saves, but because the Christ who saves sinners must be experienced personally as the foundation upon which the house of our eternal hope is built (Matthew 7:22–27; 1 Corinthians 1:30; 2:2).

Classic Reformed preachers aimed to inculcate in their hearers a spiritual discernment by which they might judge themselves and rightly apply God's Word to their cases: whether they were in the church or in the world, genuine believers or counterfeits, babes in Christ or maturing Christians.[14] Archibald Alexander (1772–1851) said,

> The promises and threatenings contained in the Scriptures [must] be applied to the characters to which they properly belong. How often do we hear a preacher expatiating on the rich consolations of the exceeding great and precious promises of God, when no mortal can tell, from anything

which he says, to whom they are applicable. In much of preaching, there is a vague and indiscriminate application of the special promises of the covenant of grace, as though all who heard them were true Christians, and had a claim to the comfort which they offer.

Alexander lamented how rare such discriminating preaching had become in the early nineteenth century, saying, "In the best days of the reformed churches, such discriminating delineation of character, by the light of Scripture, formed an important part of almost every sermon."[15]

5. Piety Energized with Idealism, Realism, and Optimism

When leaving active duty of the United States Army, my boss said to me, "Son, you need to remember three things if you ever get called by Uncle Sam to fight in a war: first, remember how a war ought to go—you've been trained for that, so don't lose your idealism; second, remember that wars never go the way they are supposed to go—they are always more complex and bloody than you might think, so don't lose a sense of realism; and third, remember your end goal—you are fighting for this great and strong country, so don't lose your sense of optimism that you will prevail in the end." Later, I have often used this advice as an illustration to young ministers on how they should preach experientially. Experiential preaching involves expounding the Christian life idealistically (think of Romans 8), realistically (think of Romans 7:14–25), and optimistically, anticipating ultimate victory in the end (think of Revelation 21). If a minister preaches the Christian life only idealistically, some genuine Christians will feel so overwhelmed with their own inadequacy that they will wonder if they are Christians at all. If a minister preaches the Christian life only realistically, Christians will be prone to be remain satisfied with where they are at spiritually despite their battles with indwelling sin. And if a minister neglects preaching optimistically about future glory with Christ in the realm of celestial bliss where war is no more, Christians will be stripped of much of their experiential, eschatological hope.

Thus, the piety of Reformed Christianity has the perspective of a soldier in a violent battle when the overall war is already won. William Gurnall (1616–1679) described Christianity as "a war between the saint and Satan, and that so bloody a one, that the cruellest which ever was fought by men, will be found but sport and child's play to this."[16] Consequently, Reformed experiential piety is idealistic, realistic, and optimistic.

Piety is idealistic when it knows how matters *ought* to go in their lives (Romans 6:1–23; 8:1–17). Willem Teellinck (1579–1629) said, "True godliness shows itself...[when] one makes a sincere resolve, and comes to a firm decision, to walk from henceforth in all the ways of the Lord, always making God's good, acceptable, and perfect will a rule of life, and making God's glory the chief end of all one does."[17]

Piety is realistic insofar as it understands how matters *actually* go in the lives of God's people (Romans 7:14–25; 8:18–27). The Heidelberg Catechism (Q. 114) confesses: "Even the holiest men, while in this life have only a small beginning of this obedience." Christianity is a struggle, a hard fight for eternal life (Ephesians 6:12; 1 Timothy 6:12). Christians often find themselves disappointed and discouraged, especially with themselves. Gurnall said, "Cowards never won heaven."[18]

And piety is optimistic because it holds to an assured hope of how matters ultimately *will* go for God's people, for they are more than conquerors in Christ Jesus (Romans 8:28–39). Calvin said, "The goodness of God never fails."[19]

In sum, all three—idealism, realism, and optimism—are essential. Telling how matters *do* go without indicating how they *should* go allows the believer to cease from pressing forward to grow in the grace and knowledge of Christ (2 Peter 3:18). Only telling how matters should go rather than how they do go may deprive the believer of the assurance that the Lord has worked in his heart. Dwelling on the hard realities of this present age will dampen the believer's hope of seeing Christ coming again in glory. But the combination of idealism, realism, and optimism encourages him to leave the past behind, and "press toward the mark for the prize of the high calling of God in Christ Jesus" (Philippians 3:14).

6. Piety Rooted in Heart Knowledge

Reformed theologians have always stressed the importance of knowledge for godliness. As noted above, Calvin defined "piety" as "that reverence joined with love of God which the knowledge of his benefits induces."[20] Yet this knowledge must not be, as Calvin says, "that knowledge which, content with empty speculation, merely flits in the brain," but that which is fruitful because "it takes root in the heart."[21] The Holy Spirit "enflames our hearts with the love of God."[22]

The old Calvinistic preachers were fond of stressing the difference between head knowledge and heart knowledge in Christian faith. Head knowledge is not enough for true religion; it also demands heart knowledge. Proverbs 4:23 says, "Keep thy heart with all diligence; for out of it are the issues of life." Romans 10:10 adds, "For with the heart man believeth unto righteousness." It is one thing to know that Christ died for sinners, and another to know that He died for your sins.

Heart knowledge of God results from an experiential encounter with the Christ of Scripture through the wondrous work of the Spirit. Such knowledge transforms the heart and bears heavenly fruit. It pierces the soul with conviction of sin and unbelief (Hebrews 4:11–13). It causes the believer to savor the Lord and delight in Him (Psalm 34:8). It engenders an appetite for God's truth. As Jeremiah says, "Thy words were found, and I did eat them; and thy word was unto me the joy and rejoicing of mine heart" (Jeremiah 15:16). Heart knowledge does not lack head knowledge, but head knowledge may lack heart knowledge. The seed of heart knowledge must be planted by the Holy Spirit in the soil of head knowledge.

7. Piety Fruitful in Holy Love

Reformed experiential piety is not self-absorbed, but oriented upward in love to God and outward in love to others. It is not experience for the sake of experience, but experience for the sake of the glory of God and the good of human beings. J. I. Packer argues that the Puritans were not interested in tracing the experience of the Spirit's work in their souls to promote their own experience, but to be driven out of themselves into Christ, in whom they could then enter into fellowship with the triune God of love.[23]

Calvin articulated this principle beautifully. Earlier, I quoted Calvin's poetic statement that "we are God's," and therefore must "live for him." It is important to know that Calvin prefaced this by the principle of self-denial, by saying, "We are not our own: let not our reason nor our will, therefore, sway our plans and deeds. We are not our own: let us therefore not set it as our goal to seek what is expedient for us according to our flesh. We are not our own: in so far as we can, let us therefore forget ourselves and all that is ours."[24]

What does this mean in our relationships with our fellow human beings? Calvin quoted the apostle Paul to remind us that love is patient and kind; it does not seek its own (1 Corinthians 13:4–5). Whatever good things God has given to us are not for us alone, Calvin said, but for "the common good" as we share them with others, especially with fellow members of the body of Christ.[25] The Reformed ethic of self-denial is not stoic inhumanity or dualistic asceticism, but compassionate service to others in body and soul. Perkins said, "Mercy is a holy compassion of heart, whereby a man is moved to help another in his misery."[26] Everyone must fulfill his calling with mercy to others: the civil magistrate in his government, the minister in his preaching, the businessman in his stewardship and charity, and the employee in his conscientious work.[27]

Conclusion: The Preacher's Imperative

The practical holiness of true piety that is other-person centered places a special demand upon the preacher. John Boys (1571–1625) captured this truth when he quipped, "He doth preach most, that doth live best."[28] Do we think that we will ignite others with the love of God if we are not burning and shining lights ourselves? John Owen (1616–1683) said that a minister needs an "experience of the power of the things we preach to others." Owen wrote, "No man preaches that sermon so well to others who does not preach it first to his own heart.... Unless he finds the power of it in his own heart, he cannot have any ground of confidence that it will have power in the hearts of others."[29]

CONCLUSION

Reformed piety, exemplified in the writing of Calvin and expressed through centuries of preaching and living the Word, seeks to weave together its covenantal and experiential emphases into a seamless garment of truth and godliness. The result, when God blesses His Word, is a piety that sustains our life in biblical balance, gospel power, and spiritual richness.

Reformed piety engages people both in a personal response to God's Word and in communal relationships under the triune God. As piety of the Word, it embraces both gospel and law, both the warm relationship established in Christ and the vital obedience empowered by the Spirit. Its communal dynamic guards against self-absorbed mysticism and morbid introspection, and its discriminatory preaching protects against the dangerous presumption that outward participation in a Christian family and church equates to salvation.

Covenantal preaching and teaching that deemphasizes experiential preaching and teaching is prone to produce congregations where all the children grow up under the assumption that they are saved even if they do not show the fruits that they are. Experiential preaching and teaching that ignores covenantal preaching and teaching can easily slip into a misguided experientialism that ends in spiritual experiences rather than in Christ. That can lead, consciously or unconsciously, to a kind of presumptive "unregeneration" in which there is little expectation for the Lord to work along covenantal lines in the church. The Christian church today needs both emphases in balance to promote a robust Reformed piety.

Biblically balanced piety follows the Reformation track of gospel holiness. *Contra* nominalism, it demands the application of biblical truth to the practical life, or all is in vain. *Contra* formalism, its experiential discernment exposes the hypocrite and commends heart knowledge of God. *Contra* antinomianism, its ethical dimensions mark off authentic Christian living with the rule of the Ten Commandments. *Contra* legalism, its evangelical theology flies the banner of salvation by grace alone through faith alone in Christ alone. Reformed piety must always be profoundly theological because of its roots in the knowledge of God.

Although the term "piety" today may suggest a folding of the hands in quietistic devotion, Reformed piety stirs Christians up to love and good works. Personal devotion and public worship drive a life of service according to each person's gifts, place, and vocation. The motivating force and essential nature of holiness is love: supreme, adoring love for God and compassionate love for our fellow human sinners and sufferers. Reformed piety does not honor mavericks who relish their independence and autonomy, but empowers the life of the body where each member gives and receives grace in mutual interdependence and common subordination to the Lord.

The constant motion of holiness presses the godly into warfare against Satan and indwelling sin. Reformed experiential preaching equips the saints in Christ for this battle. It imparts to them the high ideals of the Christian life after which growing Christians constantly strive. It cautions them with the gritty realism of human folly and sin that remain in the best of believers. And it lifts their eyes to see Christ, now seated at God's right hand and one day coming on the clouds of heaven.

Thus, Reformed piety is the godliness of pilgrims who are running the race set before them, looking to Jesus as they pass through this spiritual wilderness on their way to the glories of the celestial city. It is a piety of enduring faith and unshakeable hope, and contains within itself the very spark of heaven.

NOTES

Introduction

1. This book is an expansion of a plenary, keynote address that I (Joel Beeke) gave for the International Council of Reformed Churches (ICRC), in Jordan, Ontario, on July 11, 2017, as well as from the annual Martyn-Lloyd-Jones Memorial Lecture which I delivered at London Seminary in England on October 17, 2018. I am grateful for both of these invitations.

1. Calvin's Piety

1. John Calvin, *Institutes of the Christian Religion*, ed. John T. McNeill and trans. Ford Lewis Battles (Philadelphia: Westminster Press, 1960), 1.1.1; 1.2.1. Hereafter cited as Calvin, *Inst.* Some of the material in this section is condensed from Joel R. Beeke, "Calvin on piety," in *The Cambridge Companion to Calvin,* ed. Donald K. McKim (Cambridge: Cambridge University Press, 2004), 125–52.
2. Cited in John Hesselink, "The Development and Purpose of Calvin's Institutes," in *Articles on Calvin and Calvinism, vol. 4, Influences upon Calvin and Discussion of the 1559 Institutes,* ed. Richard C. Gamble (New York: Garland, 1992), 215–16.
3. See Brian A. Gerrish, "Theology within the Limits of Piety Alone: Schleiermacher and Calvin's Doctrine of God," in *Reformatio Perennis: Essays on Calvin and the Reformation in Honor of Ford Lewis Battles,* ed. B. A. Gerrish and Robert Benedetto, Pittsburgh Theological Monograph Series (Eugene, Ore.: Pickwick, 1981), 67–87; reprinted in B. A. Gerrish, *The Old Protestantism and the New: Essays on the Reformation Heritage* (London: T and T Clark, 1982), 196–207.
4. Calvin, *Inst.,* pref. add. sec. 1.
5. John T. White, *The White Latin Dictionary* (Chicago: Follett Publishing, 1929), 467.
6. Cf. Lucien Joseph Richard, *The Spirituality of John Calvin* (Atlanta: John Knox Press, 1974), 100–101; Sou-Young Lee, "Calvin's Understanding of *Pietas,*" in *Calvinus Sincerioris Religionis Vindex,* ed. W. H. Neuser and B. G. Armstrong (Kirksville, Mo.: Sixteenth-Century Studies, 1997), 226–33; H. W. Simpson, "*Pietas* in the *Institutes* of Calvin," *Reformational Tradition: A Rich Heritage and Lasting Vocation* (Potchefstroom, South Africa: Potchefstroom University for Christian Higher Education, 1984), 179–91.
7. Calvin, *Inst.,* 1.2.1.
8. Calvin, *Inst.,* 3.19.2.

9. Calvin, *Inst.*, 3.2.1; John Calvin, *Ioannis Calvini opera quae supersunt omnia*, ed. Wilhelm Baum, Edward Cunitz, and Edward Reuss, *Corpus Reformatorum*, vols. 29–87 (Brunsvigae: C.A. Schwetschke and Son, 1863–1900), 43:428, 47:316. Hereafter cited as *CO*.

10. *CO* 26:693.

11. Calvin, *Inst.*, 3.7.1.

12. *CO* 49:51.

13. *CO* 26:166, 33:186, 47:377–78, 49:245, 51:21.

14. Latin: *Cor meum tibi offero, Domine, prompte et sincere.*

15. Willem van 't Spijker, "*Extra nos* and *in nos* by Calvin in a Pneumatological Light," in *Calvin and the Holy Spirit*, ed. Peter DeKlerk (Grand Rapids: Calvin Studies Society, 1989), 39–62; Merwyn S. Johnson, "Calvin's Ethical Legacy," in *The Legacy of John Calvin*, ed. David Foxgrover (Grand Rapids: Calvin Studies Society, 2000), 63–83.

16. Calvin, *Inst.*, 3.2.24; John Calvin, *Commentaries* (Calvin Translation Society; repr., Grand Rapids: Baker, 2003), on 1 John 2:12. Hereafter cited as *Commentary*.

17. Calvin, *Inst.*, 3.11.1.

18. John Calvin, *Sermons on Galatians*, trans. Kathy Childress (Edinburgh: Banner of Truth Trust, 1997), 2:17–18.

19. Calvin, *Inst.*, 4.1.4–5.

20. Calvin, *Commentary* on Romans 12:6.

21. Calvin, *Commentary* on 1 Corinthians 12:12.

22. John Calvin, *Sermons of M. John Calvin, on the Epistles of S. Paule to Timothie and Titus*, trans. L. T. (1579; repr. facsimile, Edinburgh: Banner of Truth, 1983), 1 Timothy 1:8–11.

23. John Calvin, *Calvin: Theological Treatises*, ed. J. K. S. Reid (Philadelphia: Westminster Press, 1954), 173. Cf. Brian Armstrong, "The Role of the Holy Spirit in Calvin's Teaching on the Ministry," *Calvin and the Holy Spirit*, ed. P. DeKlerk (Grand Rapids: Calvin Studies Society, 1989), 99–111.

24. Calvin, *Inst.*, 4.14.1.

25. John Walchenbach, "The Influence of David and the Psalms on the Life and Thought of John Calvin" (Th.M. thesis, Pittsburgh Theological Seminary, 1969).

26. *CO* 31:19; translation taken from Barbara Pitkin, "Imitation of David: David as a Paradigm for Faith in Calvin's Exegesis of the Psalms," *Sixteenth-Century Journal* 24, no. 4 (1993): 847.

27. This section was first translated into English in 1549 as *The Life and Conversation of a Christian Man* and has been reprinted often as *The Golden Booklet of the True Christian Life*. More recently, it is has been freshly translated and edited by Aaron Clay Denlinger and Burk Parsons as *A Little Book on the Christian Life* (Orlando, Fla.: Reformation Trust, 2017).

28. Cf. Erroll Hulse, "The Preacher and Piety," in *The Preacher and Preaching*, ed. Samuel T. Logan, Jr. (Phillipsburg, N.J.: Presbyterian and Reformed, 1986), 71.

29. Calvin, *Inst.*, 2.10.1.

2. Covenantal Piety

1. Johannes Cocceius, *The Doctrine of the Covenant and Testament of God*, trans. Casey Carmichael (1660; Grand Rapids: Reformation Heritage Books, 2016), 22.

2. Westminster Confession of Faith, 7.1, in *Westminster Confession of Faith* (1646; Glasgow: Free Presbyterian Publications, 1994), 41.

3. John Murray, *The Covenant of Grace: A Biblico-Theological Study* (Phillipsburg, N.J.: P&R, 1953), 17–20.

4. E.g.,Walter Marshall, *The Gospel Mystery of Sanctification* (1692; Grand Rapids: Reformation Heritage Books, 1999).

5. Jean Taffin, *The Marks of God's Children*, trans. Peter Y. De Jong (1585; Grand Rapids: Baker Academic, 2003). Also, see John Flavel, *Preparations for Suffering* (1681) in *The Works of John Flavel*, Vol. 6 (Edinburgh: Banner of Truth, 1968); Thomas Boston, *The Crook in the Lot* (1737) in *Complete Works of Thomas Boston*, Vol. 3 (Stoke-on-Trent, U.K.: Tentmaker Publications, 2002); Brian Cosby, *Suffering and Sovereignty* (Grand Rapids: Reformation Heritage Books, 2012). On adoption more generally, see John Girardeau, "The Doctrine of Adoption" in *Discussions of Theological Questions* (1905; Harrisonburg, Va.: Sprinkle, 1986); John Murray, "Adoption" in *Collected Writings of John Murray*, Vol. 2 (Edinburgh: Banner of Truth, 1977); Joel Beeke, *Heirs with Christ: The Puritans on Adoption* (Grand Rapids: Reformation Heritage Books, 2008); David Garner, *Sons in the Son* (Phillipsburg, N.J.: P&R, 2016).

6. Richard Sibbes, *The Love of Christ* (1639 as *Bowels Opened*; repr., Edinburgh, Banner of Truth, 2011); Samuel Rutherford, *Letters of Samuel Rutherford* (1664 as *Joshua Redivivus*; repr., Edinburgh: Banner of Truth, 2006).

7. James Guthrie, *The Christian's Great Interest* (1658; Edinburgh: Banner of Truth, 1969), 169–92; Ebenezer Erskine, personal covenants written c. 1713, in Donald Fraser, *The Life and Diary of the Rev. Ebenezer Erskine* (Edinburgh: William Oliphant, 1831), 113–23.

8. Francis Turretin, *Institutes of Elenctic Theology*, trans. George Giger, ed. James T. Dennison, Jr. (1679–1685; Phillipsburg, N.J.: P&R, 1992), 2:138 (11.22.7). See also Girolamo Zanchi, *Confession of Christian Religion*, ed. Luca Baschera and Christian Moser (1599; Leiden, The Netherlands : Brill, 2007), 1:191; Herman Witsius, *The Economy of the Covenants between God and Man* (1677; Kingsburg, Calif.: Den Dulk Christian Foundation, 1990), 1:63; John Dick, *Lectures on Theology* (Philadelphia: J Whetham and Son, 1841), 2:523; John L. Mackay, *Exodus* (Ross-shire, Scotland: Mentor, 2001), 340–41 (on Ex. 20:1).

9. Latent here is the typical Reformed threefold division of the law into moral, ceremonial, and judicial. See, for example, Zanchi, *Confession*, 1.189; Turretin, *Institutes*, 2.145–46 (11.24.1–3); Philip Ross, *From the Finger of God: The Biblical and Theological Basis for the Threefold Division of the Law* (Ross-shire, Scotland: Mentor, 2010).

10. Robert Rollock, *A Treatise of God's Effectual Calling* (1597) in *Select Works of Robert Rollock*, Vol. 1 (Grand Rapids: Reformation Heritage Books, 2008);

Zanchi, *Confession*, 1:191; Coccerius, *The Doctrine of the Covenant and Testament of God*, 28–31; Witsius, *The Economy of the Covenants*, 1:60–71; Turretin, *Institutes*, 2:1–167; Dick, *Lectures on Theology*, 2:513, 522; O. Palmer Robertson, *The Christ of the Covenants* (Phillipsburg, N.J.: P&R, 1980), 167–99.

11. This is contrary to at least two other interpretations of Sinai: (1) that God was giving a law for self-justification (typically, a dispensationalist view); (2) that God was giving a temporary law intended only for the Old Testament theocracy and focused on the obtaining and retention of the land of Canaan (e.g., Michael Horton, *God of Promise* [Grand Rapids: Baker, 2006], 35–76; Peter Gentry and Stephen Wellum, *Kingdom through Covenant: A Biblical-Theological Understanding of the Covenants* [Wheaton, Ill.: Crossway, 2012], 327, 354–56).

12. Zanchi, *Confession*, 1:191; Matthew Poole, *A Commentary on the Holy Bible*, Volume 1 (1685; Peabody, Mass.: Hendrickson, 2010), 158 (on Ex. 20:2); Mackay, *Exodus*, 342 (on Ex. 20:2).

13. Melanchthon's doctrine in this area showed marked development in the 1520s and 1530s. See Timothy J. Wengert, *Law and Gospel: Philip Melanchthon's Debate with John Agricola of Eisleben over Poenitentia* (Grand Rapids: Baker Academic, 1997). For an example of the ongoing Lutheran debate on these issues, see *Concordia Theological Quarterly* 69, no. 3–4 (July/October 2005).

14. Calvin, *Inst.*, 3.7.12.

15. Edward Fisher, *The Marrow of Modern Divinity* (1645; Ross-shire, Scotland: Christian Focus, 2009).

16. Thomas Schreiner, *40 Questions about Christians and Biblical Law* (Grand Rapids: Kregel, 2010), 67–107, esp. 97–107. See also Gentry and Wellum, *Kingdom through Covenant*, 354–56; Michael Horton, *The Law of Perfect Freedom* (Chicago: Moody, 1993), 20–33; *The Christian Faith* (Grand Rapids: Zondervan, 2011), 136–39, 677–80; Jason Meyer, *The End of the Law: Mosaic Covenant in Pauline Theology* (Nashville: B&H, 2009); Albert Mohler, *Words from the Fire: Hearing the Voice of God in the Ten Commandments* (Chicago: Moody, 2009), 29–37.

17. Heidelberg Catechism (1563), Questions 91–115; Samuel Bolton, *The True Bounds of Christian Freedom* (1645; Edinburgh: Banner of Truth, 1964); Westminster Larger Catechism (1647), Q. 91–149, in *Westminster Confession of Faith*, 178–238; James Durham, *A Practical Exposition of the Ten Commandments* (1676 as *The Law Unsealed*; Dallas: Naphtali, 2002); Thomas Watson, *The Ten Commandments* (1692 as part of *A Body of Practical Divinity*; Edinburgh: Banner of Truth, 1965).

18. J. Douma, *The Ten Commandments: Manual for the Christian Life*, trans. Nelson Kloosterman (Phillipsburg, N.J.: P&R, 1996); Philip Ryken, *Written in Stone: The Ten Commandments and Today's Moral Crisis* (Phillipsburg, N.J.: P&R, 2003); J. I. Packer, *Keeping the Ten Commandments* (Wheaton, Ill.: Crossway, 2007); John Frame, *The Doctrine of the Christian Life* (Phillipsburg, N.J.: P&R, 2008); 385–850. For a different version of the same approach, see John Murray, *Principles of Conduct* (London: Tyndale Press, 1957).

19. Robert Bruce, *The Mystery of the Lord's Supper* (1590; Ross-shire, Scotland:

Christian Focus, 2005); George Gillespie, *Aaron's Rod Blossoming* (1646; Harrisonburg, Va.: Sprinkle, 1985), 223–59; James Durham, *Concerning Scandal* (1680; Dallas: Naphtali Press, 1990); John Willison, *A Sacramental Catechism* (1720; Morgan, Pa.: Soli Deo Gloria, 2000); James Bannerman, *The Church of Christ* (1869; Edinburgh: Banner of Truth, 2015); Brian Habig and Les Newsom, *The Enduring Community: Embracing the Priority of the Church* (Jackson, Miss.: Reformed University Press, 2001).

20. Westminster Larger Catechism, Q. 118; Durham, *Concerning Scandal,* 221–26; Matthew Henry, *An Exposition of the Old and New Testament,* Vol. 1 (1708–1710; New York: Fleming H. Revell, n.d.), on Ex. 20:10.

21. Calvin, *Commentary* on Genesis 17:7.

22. Turretin, *Institutes,* 3:414–20 (19.20); John Murray, *Christian Baptism* (Phillipsburg, N.J.: P&R, 1980); *The Case for Covenantal Infant Baptism,* ed. Gregg Strawbridge (Phillipsburg, N.J.: P&R, 2003).

23. Durham, *Concerning Scandal,* 221–36; Jacobus Koelman, *The Duties of Parents* (1679; Grand Rapids: Reformation Heritage Books, 2012); Matthew Henry, "A Church in the House" (1704) in *The Complete Works of Matthew Henry* (Grand Rapids: Baker, 1979), 1:248–67; Joel Beeke, *Family Worship* (Grand Rapids: Reformation Heritage Books, 2009); Jason Helopoulos, *A Neglected Grace: Family Worship in the Christian Home* (Ross-shire, Scotland: Christian Focus, 2013); Terry Johnson, *The Family Worship Book* (Ross-shire, Scotland: Christian Focus, 2009).

24. Tobias Crisp, *Christ Alone Exalted* (1643; Createspace, 2016); John Saltmarsh, *Free Grace* (1646; Southampton: Huntingtonian Press, 2000); Tullian Tchividjian, *Jesus + Nothing = Everything* (Wheaton, Ill.: Crossway, 2011). See the critical analyses in *Sanctification: Growing in Grace,* ed. Joseph Pipa (Greenville, S.C.: Southern Presbyterian Press, 2001), 129–78; Mark Jones, *Antinomianism: Reformed Theology's Unwelcome Guest?* (Phillipsburg, N.J.: P&R, 2013).

25. Zanchi, *Confession,* 1:197–99; Hans Boersma, *A Hot Pepper Corn: Richard Baxter's Doctrine of Justification in Its Seventeenth-Century Context* (Vancouver, B.C.: Regent College Publishing, 2003).

26. Guy Prentiss Waters, *The Federal Vision and Covenant Theology: A Comparative Analysis* (Phillipsburg, N.J.: P&R, 2006).

3. Experiential Piety

1. For several thoughts in this section, I am indebted to an address by Ian Hamilton on "Experimental Preaching" at the 2004 Banner of Truth Conference in Grantham, Pa. Some parts are also revised from my "Reformed Experiential Preaching" in *Feed My Sheep: A Passionate Plea for Preaching* (Morgan, Pa.: Soli Deo Gloria, 2002), 94–128; *Puritan Evangelism: A Biblical Approach* (Grand Rapids: Reformation Heritage Books, 2007); *Living for God's Glory: An Introduction to Calvinism* (Orlando: Reformation Trust, 2008); and *Reformed Preaching: Proclaiming God's Word from the Heart of the Preacher to the Heart of His People* (Wheaton, Ill.: Crossway, 2018).

2. Paul Helm, "Christian Experience," *Banner of Truth*, no. 139 (April 1975): 6.

3. Calvin, *Inst.*, 1.6.2.

4. Calvin, *Inst.*, 1.6.3.

5. Lionel Greve, "Freedom and Discipline in the Theology of John Calvin, William Perkins and John Wesley: An Examination of the Origin and Nature of Pietism" (PhD Dissertation, Hartford Seminary Foundation, 1975), 273.

6. William Perkins, *Works of William Perkins* (London: John Legatt, 1613), 2:762.

7. Cotton Mather, *Manuductio ad ministerium: Directions for a Candidate to the Ministry* (New York: AMS Press, 1978), 16.

8. Calvin, *Commentary* on John 17:3.

9. Robert Burns, introduction to *Works of Thomas Halyburton* (London: Thomas Tegg, 1835), xiv–xv.

10. Charles Bridges, *The Christian Ministry* (Edinburgh: Banner of Truth, 2006), 275.

11. *Westminster Confession of Faith*, 380.

12. *Westminster Confession of Faith*, 380.

13. Heidelberg Catechism, Q. 83, in *The Three Forms of Unity* (Birmingham, Ala.: Solid Ground Christian Books, 2010), 97.

14. Bridges, *The Christian Ministry*, 277–80.

15. Archibald Alexander, in *The Princeton Pulpit*, ed. John T. Duffield (New York: Charles Scribner, 1852), 40–42.

16. William Gurnall, *The Christian in Complete Armour*, 2 vols. in 1 (1662–1665; Edinburgh: Banner of Truth, 1964), 1:2.

17. Willem Teellinck, *The Path of True Godliness*, trans. Annemie Godbehere, ed. Joel R. Beeke, Classics of Reformed Spirituality (Grand Rapids: Reformation Heritage Books, 2003), 32–33.

18. Gurnall, *The Christian in Complete Armour*, 1:16.

19. Calvin, *Commentary* on Ps. 23:6.

20. Calvin, *Inst.*, 1.2.1.

21. Calvin, *Inst.*, 1.5.9.

22. Calvin, *Inst.*, 3.1.3.

23. J. I. Packer, *A Quest for Godliness: The Puritan Vision of the Christian Life* (Wheaton, Ill.: Crossway, 1990), 117–18; "The Puritan Idea of Communion with God," in *Press toward the Mark*, Puritan and Reformed Studies Conference, 1961 (London: n.p., 1962), 7.

24. Calvin, *Inst.*, 3.7.1.

25. Calvin, *Inst.*, 3.7.5.

26. William Perkins, *An Exposition of Christ's Sermon on the Mount*, in *The Works of William Perkins, Volume 1*, ed. J. Stephen Yuille (Grand Rapids: Reformation Heritage Books, 2014), 198 (on Matt. 5:7).

27. Perkins, *Sermon on the Mount*, in *Works*, 1:201 (on Matt. 5:7).

28. John Boys, *The Works of John Boys: An Exposition of the Several Offices* (New York: Stanford and Swords, 1851), 25.

29. John Owen, *The Duty of a Pastor*, in *The Works of John Owen*, ed. William H. Goold (New York: Robert Carter & Brothers, 1851), 9:455.